Part of the "NEARBY" series of books.

THE LIBRARY

Part of the "NEARBY" series of books.
BY: DA BUTLER

It was a rainy Saturday. Arthur and Andy had just finished eating their lunch and because of the rain, they couldn't go out and play in their sandbox. They weren't sure what to do next.

Just then their mother walked into the kitchen and asked the boys if they wanted to go to their local library. Arthur and Andy had never been to the library and they were very excited.

Arthur and Andy's mother said that there would be a storytime at one o'clock so they put on their raincoats and rubber boots. The Library was a few blocks away and the boys had fun splashing in the puddles along the way.

When they arrived at the library the librarian showed them where to hang up their wet coats.

"Welcome to the library," she said, "storytime is about to start."

She directed them to a corner of the library with comfortable couches and big large pillows on the floor.

"Hello everyone, my name is Michael. Come in and make yourself comfortable. I am going to read a story today about dragons!"

All of the children smiled and giggled because dragon stories were always exciting.

Arthur and Andy found a seat and listened carefully to Michael. They enjoyed the story so much that after the story was over they asked their mom if they could buy the book to take home.

"That is the great thing about the library boys, you don't have to buy books here, you can borrow them and bring them back when you're done!" said mom.

"We can borrow any book in this whole library?" Andy asked.

"Yes, but first you need to get a library card. Let's go and see the librarian that you met when we first came in."

"Hello," said Arthur, "can you help us get a library card, please?"

The librarian smiled at the boys. "Of course, I would be happy to help you both. Getting a library card is a great start to learning about so many things and places. There are thousands of books here and you can now borrow any that you want."

The librarian presented the boys with their very first library cards. "If you need any help finding a book please come and ask me."

The boys started to look up and down the aisles of the children's section. There were so many books to choose from. There were picture books, storybooks, and even movies to borrow.

The boys each took two books to the front desk and the friendly librarian helped them check the books out. They were so excited to get home and read their new books. One of them was the book about dragons that they heard at storytime.

The librarian told Arthur and Andy that there were a lot of activities and events at the library. Sometimes there are crafts and games, but right now, down the hall, there was a puppet show about to start.

"Mommy, mommy, can we go and watch the show?" asked Arthur

"Please mommy!" pleaded Andy.

"Of course we can, let's go!

Arthur and Andy sat in the front row for the puppet show. They smiled and laughed at the funny puppets and Arthur and Andy couldn't believe how much fun it was to visit the library.

The rain had finally stopped. The boys said goodbye to the librarian and walked back home with their new books in their arms and their brand new library cards in their pockets.

More titles in the NEARBY series:

The Backyard
The Fire Station
The Farm

Other DA BUTLER titles:

My Glasses
Freckles!
My Daddy
Kindness
Forever Friend
The New Baby

www.ingramcontent.com/pod-product-compliance
Lightning Source LLC
Chambersburg PA
CBHW042051050526
44107CB00109B/1059